How to Build and Maintain Recovery:

A Positive Approach to Addiction Recovery

Gary Blanchard, MA, LADC1

© 2014 by Gary Blanchard

ISBN 978-0615972060
LCCN 2014903175

Also by Gary Blanchard:
Positive Path Recovery: A Clinician's Guide
Counseling for Medication Assisted Recovery

Positive Path Books
West Brookfield, MA

www.garyblanchard.net

Acknowledgements

There are many people who have influenced my approach to addictions treatment. Bill W. and Dr. Bob, the founders of Alcoholics Anonymous, helped develop the modern approach to addiction treatment. Their wisdom plays a large part in turning people's lives around and deeply informs this approach. Terrence Gorski, known for his work on relapse prevention, is the source of the idea that inspired the Building Recovery concept. Dr. Albert Ellis, who developed Rational Emotive Behavior Therapy, has provided a valuable tool to help others overcome addiction. I also owe a lot to my co-workers and clients over the past years for their insights, openness, and honesty. They have all been a part of the exploration and insight that informs this book.

Most of all, I want to thank and acknowledge my wife, Carol Mays. Without her, none of this would have happened. Her love and support have helped to make me who I am today. Words cannot express how much she means to me.

Table Of Contents

Introduction.. 9
Focus on the Positive.................................... 11
Recovery Is More Than Not Using Alcohol and
Drugs.. 13
Relapse is More Than Drug Use...................... 15
Starting the Recovery Process........................ 17
Principle 1.. 21
Principle 2.. 25
Principle 3.. 33
Principle 4.. 37
Principle 5.. 45
Principle 6.. 53
Principle 7.. 57
Principle 8.. 67
Recovery is a Process.................................... 71
Practicing Patience....................................... 73
Progress, Not Perfection................................ 75
The Role of Goals.. 79
Reward Yourself.. 83
Staying Focused.. 87
Staying Connected....................................... 91
You Are Not Your Addiction.......................... 95
Wherever You Go, There You Are................... 97
The Importance of a Program......................... 99
Understanding Triggers................................. 101
Problem Solving.. 105
Weakening Worry.. 111
Learn From the Past..................................... 115
The Art of Being... 117
The Role of Service in Recovery..................... 119
Moving Forward.. 123
Positive Path and the Twelve Steps.................. 127
Feelings List... 133
Selected Readings.. 135

Table of Contents

Section One:

Getting Started

Introduction

I have come to believe that it is time to look at relapse in recovery in a different way. I don't mean that we have been looking at it in a wrong way, but maybe a different approach to relapse will make it easier for people who choose the path of recovery to remain successful in their effort. In this book I hope to present a number of thoughts and suggestions for building a successful, lasting recovery. These short articles each provide food for thought, or help, or encouragement, or information. I keep them short so you can easily read them as your time allows. If you put them all together, though, they do offer a different way to think about relapse, a way to move your thoughts from failure to success. I don't present any radical ideas, but these ideas can lead to radical, positive change.

As you go through this book, you will find there are some questions or exercises to help you build your recovery. I encourage you to take time and answer these. You may complete the exercises in the spaces provided in the book, or may choose to record the exercises in a separate journal.

I welcome you as you begin a new part of your recovery, a part where you think more about building your recovery and less about losing it. You deserve to have success, and you can have success.

I: Focus on the Positive

You are committed to making a major change in your life. The path of recovery is not always easy, and it is not always smooth, but it is better than the path of addiction. While you need to be aware of the possibility of relapse, you also need to think in a more positive way. If you go to the doctor for a check-up, you can think of it as building your health, or you can think of it as preventing death. While there is no change in what happens in the doctor's office, you will feel better if you think about the visit as building your health. In the same way, you can think about building your recovery or preventing relapse. You will have the same result, but you will feel better if you focus on the positive.

Too much of life is filled with negative thoughts. If you watch the news, you might believe that the world is a terrible place. Yet, if you look around, you can find so much that is good. If you focus on the bad things, you will feel bad. If you decide to focus on the good things, though, you are more likely to feel good. I am not suggesting that you go into denial and don't acknowledge the negative things in life. The negative will always be there. If you make that your focus, though, you might forget the good.

When you focus on building recovery, you focus on doing the things that make you stronger. You build skills that allow continued growth. You make connections with people who support your new life. As long as you build recovery, you will continue to eliminate the negative people, places, and things from your life. This will prevent relapse and will allow you to feel better in the process.

II: Recovery Is More Than Not Using Alcohol and Drugs

People often seem to think that recovery is no longer using alcohol and other drugs. In fact, simply not using is abstinence, not recovery. Recovery is returning to the person you were before drugs and alcohol became a major part of your life, and then becoming even better. Recovery is also undoing the damage done to your body, your thinking, and your behavior.

When you think about it, the progression of your drug use led you to become different from the person you once were. You no longer thought about life, yourself, the world, or even your values in the same way. Your life became centered on using the drug; this drug-centered thinking became ingrained and then affected your behavior.

You need to recognize that this drug-centered thinking and behavior is now so deeply ingrained that it won't just go away when you stop using alcohol and other drugs. You will need to work to eliminate the drug-centered thinking and behavior, and work to replace it with more positive, recovery-centered thinking and behavior. This process is the recovery process.

As long as you are content with simply abstaining from alcohol and drug use, you are at much greater risk of returning to it. When you start the recovery process, making the changes that support being drug-free, you are on the way to a new and better life.

III: Relapse is More Than Drug Use

You may think that relapse means that you have returned to drug use after stopping your use of drugs and alcohol. This is really only part of a relapse, and it is the final part of the relapse. To better understand this, think about how you were when you were addicted. You did things that you wouldn't think of doing when you are not using. Perhaps you lied, both to yourself and to others. You might have taken money, or sold things from around the house. Maybe you hung around people who were not good people to be around. Think about your activities when you were using. All of these things were a part of your addiction.

Once you start to work on your recovery you began to change these actions and people. At first, it may seem difficult, but you work hard at these changes. Soon, you stop paying attention to them. For a while everything is going well. Then, even though you don't notice it, you start to return to old habits or old people. This is a sign that you are in the process of relapse. If you don't recognize this and change your actions it may not be long before you return to drug use.

By learning to recognize all the ways that addiction affected your life you can begin to recognize when your recovery begins to suffer. This allows you to stop a relapse before it leads to drug use and allows you to continue to build a successful recovery.

IV: Starting The Recovery Process

There are many ways to begin the process of recovery. Perhaps the best known is the Twelve Steps of Alcoholics Anonymous. I will not say too much about this approach as so much has already been written about it, and there is little I could add to it. I will say, however, that one mistake that people often make is to assume that merely attending Twelve-Step meetings will build recovery. The fact of the matter is that the Twelve Steps are action-oriented; the power and effectiveness comes from taking action on the steps. Attending support group meetings is important, but it is only part of the recovery process.

Over time, I have developed an approach to recovering from addiction that I call *Positive Path Recovery*. This is another way of looking at the recovery process. It is not meant to replace the Twelve-Step approach, but offers some different insights and recovery tasks. Positive Path Recovery is based on Eight Principles:

1) Admit that the substance has taken control and commit to a path of recovery.
2) Redefine and rebuild the sense of self. (The true self)
3) Take responsibility and accept forgiveness for past actions.
4) Learn to identify and express feelings.
5) Improve communication with others.
6) Restore connection with significant people and make connection with others who can support recovery.

7) Identify barriers to recovery and plan to overcome them.
8) Let Go!

Each of these Principles will be explored in the next eight chapters of the book. From there, we will explore more ways to build recovery.

Section Two:

The Principles of Positive Path Recovery

V: Principle #1
Admit that the substance has taken control and commit to a path of recovery.

An old saying states that every journey begins with a single step. The Positive Path begins when a person admits that they have lost control over their use of mood-altering substances. As we have seen, sometimes it is not easy to make this admission. Once you have made it, however, you are on your way to recovery.

At this point I would like to state that, while an admission of the problem is essential, I feel it is possible to acknowledge it in an affirming manner. Generally, a person in recovery identifies himself or herself by saying "I am an alcoholic" or I am an addict." I feel that it is much healthier to say, "I am a person who is recovering from addiction." This statement acknowledges the problem but it also acknowledges that the person is in the process of change. This is a move away from self-denigration to self-affirmation. Since low self-esteem is common among people with addictive disease, you should affirm yourself as much as possible. This is not denial--it is admitting the truth in a positive way.

The second part of this principle states a commitment to a path of recovery. It is important to realize that a commitment to recovery is the beginning of the recovery process rather than a one-time event. Once you have made this commitment, you are ready to recover the true self, the essence of your being. This will be discussed in detail in the exploration of the second principle.

The commitment to a recovery path can seem overwhelming to some people. After years of relationship with their drug (or drugs) of choice some people feel they cannot think of life without it. The key is not to think of a lifetime of abstinence; break it down into smaller, more manageable time frames. A popular phrase in recovery is "One day at a time." This is excellent advice. By telling yourself, "Today I will refrain from using any and all mood altering substances;" you have set a short-term goal that is easily reached. At first, you may find that you need to break it down into even smaller time frames. As time goes on, you may find that you expand the time frame. After a while, you may even find that you don't think about it at all.

I would like to point out that a commitment to recovery does not mean that you should not take prescribed medications. There are those who may need anti-depressants or other medication for psychological problems. These should be taken under medical supervision. Keep in mind that some of these medications may be addictive. Always tell your doctor about your history of addiction; the doctor can then prescribe medications that may be effective without the risk of addiction.

Admitting that the drug has taken control of your life and committing, on a day by day basis if necessary, to recovery is the beginning of your journey of recovery. Here are some questions that might help you in this process:

What are some ways that your addiction has taken control of your life?

How have you tried to take control of your addiction?

Do you plan to commit to a path or recovery?

What are you doing to overcome your addiction?

VI: Principle #2
Redefine and rebuild the sense of self. (The true self)

The process of addiction is a slow, steady erosion of your sense of who you are. This process may very well begin before you begin drug or alcohol use. While addiction may be a genetic, biological disease, at times the erosion of the self may lead to the first use of our drug of choice. Other times the use of drugs leads to this erosion. Either way, I believe that disconnection from the true self is an outcome of addiction.

Before I define the true self, it is important to understand what is meant by the term "self." In common usage, the self is actually the self-concept, the way that a person views his or her self. The self-concept has three components. The first is the physical self, which is the basis of self-concept for newborn infants. The second component is the social self, which is based on the feedback that we get from other people. This is the way that other people see us. The third component is the true self, which should be the main component of the self-concept.

What is the true self? It is the purest essence of our being. It is what makes each of us unique and wonderful. When we first enter the world, we are purely ourselves. As we go through life, our experiences influence our thoughts and behavior. We may try to conform to the needs and expectations of family and friends, the social self. This causes an uneasy feeling. Some people are aware of the problem and are able to deal with it; others try to hide from the feeling. When we hide from this uneasy feeling, a part of our true self is displaced.

Substance abuse is one way that people try to hide from the upset in their life. They find at first that the effect of the substance counteracts the uneasy feeling. Eventually, however, the substance will only add to it. The more they use, the more they will need to use. In the process, the physical self and the social self become the primary components of the self-concept. Recovery involves restoring the true self as the main part of the self-concept.

How can you redefine and rebuild your sense of self? One way is to spend some time in self-examination. The following questions can help you.

What do I believe about myself?

What do I believe about others?

What do I believe about the world around me?

What is important to me?

What moral or ethical guidelines do I feel that I must follow?

What must I have in order to feel fulfilled and at peace?

What do I want from life for myself and for others?

The answers to these questions will help reveal your true self. Another way to redefine and reconnect with the true self is through evaluating your strengths and weaknesses. Many times a person who is addicted will lose track of these. They tend to overlook what is right about themselves and will overemphasize or deny what is wrong. You need to acknowledge both so that you have a balanced view of who you are. List as many of your strengths and weaknesses as possible. Feel free to add to these lists at a later time.

My strengths are:

My weaknesses are:

There are other techniques that you can use as well. Meditation is an effective way to help redefine and rebuild the true self. While meditation is used by a number of religions, it is not necessarily a "religious" technique. The purpose of meditation in many religions is to transcend the self; here it is used to more fully connect with the self.

While there is no special way that a person should meditate, there are things you can do to make it easier. First, you should get away, as much as possible, from distractions. Since it is difficult to find pure silence in everyday life, you may want to listen to some quiet music or a recording of the ocean or another natural sound to help overcome the other noises. Allow yourself to be comfortable; it doesn't matter if you are sitting up or lying down.

Gently allow your thoughts to slow. If you find that you are thinking about everyday problems, make note of it and then try to set them aside. If thoughts of these problems are persistent, then allow yourself to choose one and examine it. You may need to address some of these problems before you are able to connect more deeply with yourself. If you are able to get beyond these everyday worries, you may find that your "inner voice" becomes audible.

We all have thoughts and messages that rest in the unconscious mind. Many times we react to them without knowing that they are there. In this type of meditation you can allow these messages to move toward your consciousness. Sometimes these messages are affirming, other times they are destructive. We will look at ways of dealing with the destructive messages as we explore Principle #4. For now, simply let yourself be aware of these thoughts and messages.

Guided visualization is another technique that can help you to reconnect with the true self. The following visualization is a centering exercise that allows you to imagine yourself making a journey into the deeper recesses of the self. Playing quiet, relaxing music can help to make this exercise more effective. You may want to quietly lead yourself through this exercise, or you may find it better to record the exercise ahead of time. I have indicated spaces where you may want to pause to allow yourself time for reflection and revelation.

Close your eyes, find a comfortable position, and begin to connect with the pattern of your breathing. (Pause) As you breathe in and out, imagine that the rhythm of your breathing is the rhythm of life. (Pause) Imagine that you are standing at the beginning of a path that leads into a deep forest, The sun is shining down through the trees, creating a pattern of light and shadow on the grassy path ahead. (Pause) At the end of the path, you can see a bright light; this is the light of the sun illuminating a beautiful garden that is in the center of the woods. (Pause) As you continue to connect with your breath, the Earth's heartbeat, begin to travel down the path, taking time to notice the beauty that surrounds you. (Pause) As you travel this path, you hear the sound of a rippling stream, distant at first, but becoming louder as you continue walking. (Pause) As you travel this path, appreciating the beauty that surrounds you, you may find obstacles that impede your progress. Take note of these obstacles, knowing that they may slow your journey; you also know that they will not prevent you from continuing on the path to your destination. (Pause) After you have identified these obstacles, move past them and continue down the path, realizing that the encountering and bypassing the obstacle has brought you closer to the clearing at the center of the forest. (Pause) You slowly approach that clearing; the warmth of the sunlight brings a sense of comfort and connection to your heart and soul. Relax in the sunlight, rejoicing in its restorative power. (Pause) Kneel at the side of the stream; notice how clear and soothing the water is. (Pause) As you look into the stream, you see a reflection of yourself; this reflection shows the beauty that is reflected from your depth. (Pause) You sit by the stream, looking at the reflection; you are filled by the warmth of the sun and by the knowledge and awareness of your inner beauty. (Pause) When you are ready, slowly move back to the path, returning to the place where you began this trip. (Pause) As you continue your return trip, you will once again pass the obstacles that you encountered earlier; make note of them, knowing that they are not as powerful now as they were when you first encountered them. (Pause) As you approach the head of the path, you once again become aware of the pattern of your breathing. (Pause) Very slowly and gently open your eyes, allowing yourself to return to the present reality.

These techniques require practice, but they are effective ways of redefining and reconnecting with the true self. Again, remember that recovery is a process rather than an event.

VII: Principle #3
Take responsibility and accept forgiveness for past actions.

Addiction is selfish by nature. The more a person needs their substance, the less they care about anything, or anyone, else. Once the process of recovery starts, a person must repair the damage that they have done during their active addiction. Taking responsibility may not erase the hurt and pain that others have felt, but it can ease that hurt and pain while it allows people to work toward better communication.

Taking responsibility for past actions is more than just saying, "I'm sorry." Taking responsibility includes taking action to right those wrongs whenever possible. In addictions treatment an emphasis is placed on "making amends." This is a vital part of the recovery process. When you actively work at correcting the wrong you have done, you are strengthening your connection to the true self. Others are healed as you heal yourself.

How can you know who you have harmed and how can you repair the damage? In some cases you are quite aware of the damage you inflicted while in active addiction. You see the hurt in the faces of family and significant people in your life. In other cases, the hurt may be less obvious. The best way to determine the extent of the damage is by having heartfelt talks with people. Explain that you were often unaware of what happened while you were in active addiction and that you want to know how your addiction affected the person. Most importantly, be ready and willing to listen to what the person has to say.

Listening to their answer may be difficult. You may not want to hear how awful you have been. An overactive sense of guilt may send you into a cycle of self-hatred. As we explore the fourth principle we will look at a way to overcome the self-talk that can prevent you from hearing what the person has to say.

You also need to ask what you can do to try to repair the damage. Your idea of appropriate action may be different from what the other person feels would be appropriate. To be effective, you need to meet the needs of the person that you have harmed.

Once you take responsibility for your actions, you must also accept forgiveness for them. The person that has been wronged may or may not offer forgiveness. Either way, you must forgive yourself. You cannot move forward if you are facing backwards. If you hold on to the guilt and shame, you will delay the recovery process.

As you were actively addicted, you probably began to store a reservoir of guilt and shame. These feelings then fed your addiction. If you began to experience them, you would turn to the substance to block them. If you hold on to that guilt and shame in recovery, you increase the likelihood that you will return to active use of substances.

On a sheet of paper, or in a journal, list some of the actions that you need to take responsibility for and list ways that you can try to correct these actions. This will allow you to practice the art of accepting responsibility and forgiveness.

I take responsibility for:

I can try to correct this by:

VIII: Principle #4
Learn to identify and express feelings.

As a person gets deeper into addiction, the main thing they consciously respond to is their drug. Feelings can get pushed aside; eventually they can wither and die. Once a person stops using chemicals, their feelings return; these feelings are often made stronger by physical or psychological withdrawal. As a person in recovery, you need to be able to recognize what you are feeling and need to be able to respond appropriately to these feelings. Sometimes you may be very aware of your feelings, but find that you don't know how to express them in an appropriate manner. At other times you may find that you are completely numb. The awareness and expression of feelings is an important part of the recovery process.

People are usually able to identify categories of feelings, such as fear, sadness, surprise, and joy. There are differing degrees and types of each of these feelings. The more accurately you can identify your feeling, the better you can respond appropriately to it. There is a list of over one hundred feelings in the rear of the book that you can refer to. This list can help you learn how to identify your feelings more accurately.

One reason that people don't respond appropriately to feelings is that they may feel that some of those feelings are "bad" or "wrong." They may have been taught that anger is bad; therefore, they try to deny their anger. They may have learned that happiness is not acceptable in their family and so they try to hide or deny that feeling. It is important to understand that feelings are not good or bad; they are simply what they are.

It is interesting that in Spanish a person doesn't say, "I am sad;" instead, they say, "I have sadness." While it is important to identify and accept feelings, you can also see the feeling as something you "have" rather than see it as a means of personal identification. You can say "I have anger" instead of saying "I am angry."

Another part of the process of identifying and expressing feelings is recognizing negative self-talk. Many people in recovery have irrational messages that affect their self-image. These may have existed before the onset of addiction or they may be a result of chemical use. These messages often prevent a person from reacting to the reality of a situation. The best indication of the existence of these messages is your behavior. If you find yourself reacting in a way that seems inappropriate to the situation or having a reaction that is out of proportion to the "triggering event," you can be sure that there is a hidden, negative message that is affecting your actions.

Albert Ellis, a founder of the cognitive-behavioral theory of psychology, believed that many behaviors that are considered inappropriate are caused by irrational negative messages that the person received in their life. He developed an "A-B-C" theory of behavior that can be viewed in the following diagram:

$$A \leftrightarrow \qquad B \qquad \leftrightarrow \quad C$$

(activating event)　(belief)　(consequence)

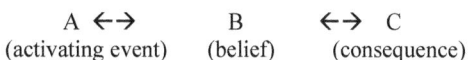

In this diagram, A is the event that eventually leads to C, the consequence of the event. The event, however, does not directly provide the consequence. It is the belief (B) about the event that causes the emotional or behavioral consequence. I do not want to overwhelm you with psychological theory, but the theory presented by Ellis does play a major part in repairing our separation from the true self.

Let me present an example of how this theory is displayed in a "real life" situation. Let's imagine that you are talking with someone who says, "I have been hurt by your actions while you were using drugs." You pull away and become angry or hurt. You are not reacting to their statement; you are reacting to deep-seated beliefs, perhaps that you are worthless and unlovable. Therefore, you react in an inappropriate manner. The problem is not that the person doesn't love you; the problem is that you don't love yourself.

A major part of identifying and expressing feelings is recognizing the underlying beliefs from your past that affect your emotions and behaviors. These beliefs affect you, no matter how deeply they are buried. You must bring them into conscious awareness so you can eliminate their power. At first, these messages elude your consciousness. You will find yourself reacting to them without being aware of their existence.

The best way to bring them into awareness is to spend time evaluating an interaction after it is over. If you or another person feels that your reaction was inappropriate, spend some time in self-examination. Ask yourself what you were thinking when you reacted. Then compare those thoughts to the event that triggered the reaction. Do the thoughts agree with the triggering event? If not, where might they have come from? How often do you have these thoughts that affected your reaction?

You may be surprised at first how often your behavior is affected by underlying beliefs rather than by actual events. As you increase your awareness of these beliefs, you will probably find that they are major hindrance to your path of recovery. I want to remind you that you should not be discouraged by the discoveries that you are making at this point.

Ellis developed an approach to disputing these messages that he called Rational Emotive Behavior Therapy (REBT). Below is an expansion of the earlier diagram, showing the REBT process:

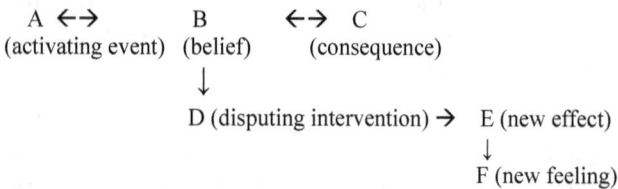

A ←→   B   ←→   C
(activating event)   (belief)   (consequence)
                   ↓

D (disputing intervention) →   E (new effect)
                                ↓
                        F (new feeling)

In this diagram, "D" is the disputing intervention; a three-step process designed to challenge the irrational beliefs. The first step in this process is detecting the irrational beliefs; especially "shoulds," "musts," "awfulizing," and "self-downing." The second part is debating these beliefs by learning how to logically question them and effectively learn to act against believing them. The third step is to learn to discriminate irrational beliefs from rational beliefs. As you learn to use the disputing intervention, you arrive at "E," an effective, rational philosophy. This philosophy helps create "F," a new set of feelings.

I know from personal experience how powerful these irrational negative messages can be. I have often found myself feeling completely hopeless and unlovable because of these messages; many times I have reacted to these messages instead of reality. I have been applying the disputing intervention to these messages and have found that they lose power with each intervention. I still have these messages, but I am learning more and more to recognize them as the irrational beliefs that they are. The use of REBT is one of the most effective tools that I have found for recovering self-esteem and eliminating irrational reactions.

The following exercise allows you to evaluate interactions to determine the belief that led to the consequence and to develop ways to dispute the belief. This format can be copied and used to evaluate any interaction that seems to be affected by hidden irrational beliefs.

Describe an event where you feel you had an inappropriate response:

What are the beliefs that you may have reacted to?

How can you dispute those beliefs?

You also need to learn how to better identify what you are feeling. There are many levels of feeling and it is good to find the best way to describe it. You may say that you feel sad; this could be anything from feeling somewhat down to feeling hopeless. When you are more accurate in your description of your feelings, you are better able to express them in an appropriate manner. Try to find words that describe levels of the following feelings:

Happy

Sad

Mad

Hurt

It is also good to recognize that feelings may sometimes be the result of feeling several things at the same time. For instance, anger may be a combination of feeling hurt, sad, disappointed, and disrespected. Select a feeling that you often feel and use the feeling list to try to determine other related feelings that may be involved.

I often feel:

Some related feelings may be:

IX: Principle #5
Improve communication with others

The fifth principle is to improve communication with others. It is ironic that people under the influence often consider themselves to be great communicators. Many people will state that relatives or friends have recorded their speech while they were under the influence; each will relate, with some surprise and embarrassment, that they didn't realize how meaningless and inarticulate they were at the time. They actually thought they were being charming and intelligent.

Many times, people with addiction problems were afraid of communicating honestly prior to the onset of their addiction. Once they give up their drug of choice they find that it is harder than they realized to talk to others, yet they also find that they need to talk with others in order to support recovery. They need to have faith in themselves and to trust that others will hear what they have to say. Rediscovering, or in many cases discovering for the first time, how to communicate with others is vitally important to maintaining sobriety.

Communication is an important part of any relationship. Effective communication requires listening skills as well as speaking skills. Before you can listen to others, however, you must be able to listen to yourself.

Many people feel that self-awareness is a selfish thing. In reality, it is vital to any type of interaction in life. Your relationship to other people, to nature, and to society is affected by your ability to know and to accept yourself.

We examined the effects of subconscious, irrational messages in the examination of the fourth principle. These messages are a major hindrance to any type of communication. The example in that chapter demonstrated how these messages affect your listening; you may hear and react to echoes from the past rather than the voice of the present. Recognizing these messages and their effects are part of the communication process.

As you are able to recognize these messages and the effect that they have, you will be increasingly able to communicate from a space beyond the effect of those messages. In some cases, it may be that you can tell the person that you are reacting to "flashes from the past;" in other cases, you may need to be able to move yourself to a space beyond those messages, or to adjust your reaction in a way that negates the power of the message. Again, the REBT process is an excellent way to deal with these situations.

Can you think of some situations when you may have reacted to what you thought was said instead of what was said?

What could you do differently to keep this from happening again?

If you have grown up to be afraid of your feelings, you may find it difficult to admit your feelings to yourself and to other people. This inability to face your feelings can be a major hindrance for communication in relationships. If, for instance, I am afraid of being rejected, I may find it difficult to express my needs to another person. In order to avoid having to share my needs and face rejection, I suppress the need, trying to pretend that it isn't there. This denial does not eliminate that need; it will surface somehow. An unexpressed and unacknowledged need, however, often reveals itself in a less than desirable fashion. It is far better to learn to express your feelings and needs than to repress them. An unexpressed need that reveals itself through inappropriate behavior causes problems that must then be discussed; the behavior adds to the problem.

You should also be aware that other people may have buried messages, and that they may or may not be aware of them. If communication is a problem, look at interactions in the relationship to see if the other person seems to be reacting to something other than the current conversation. If so, let the nature of the relationship decide your reaction to the situation. In an intimate relationship, you may want to point out that the person seems to be reacting to something other than the present situation. In less intimate relationships, it may be necessary to make allowances for the person's actions.

Cultural differences can also affect communication style and understandings. While men and women may not be from separate planets, their social training is usually different. Women may be raised to value specific traits, such as openness and vulnerability; men are often taught that these traits are signs of weakness. Racial, economic, and social differences can also result in differing values and understandings. When communication in a relationship seems blocked, it may be the result of such differences. Again, in a more intimate relationship, or in a necessary relationship, it is important for the people involved to talk about these issues and to try to come to mutual understanding. In more superficial relationships, it may be best to make allowances and try to move on.

There are ways to improve communication. One is to stay as positive as the situation permits. Avoid name-calling, sarcasm, threats, and intimidation. If you are talking about a behavior you don't like, attack the behavior, not the person. When possible, offer suggestions for solutions to a problem. Use the "sandwich" method when presenting information that could be perceived as negative; say something positive, offer the correction, then follow it with a positive statement. For example, you might say, "You have been very supportive of my recovery. I wish you could be more patient with my progress. I know you are doing your best to be understanding."

Using the techniques listed above, try to find a better way to say the following:

You are just a nag.

Do you want to call me that again? Are you ready for the consequence?

I wish you would stop leaving things around the house.

It makes me mad that you don't trust me.

Another way to improve communication is by being clear and specific. Make your point clearly; ask for what you want and tell how you feel. Avoid saying that a person "always" or "never" does something. If you are going to quote what someone said, be accurate. If you are talking about someone's actions, give specific times and examples. Avoid exaggeration, and stick to what is relevant.

It is important to talk from your own point of view. Avoid saying things like, "You just think that..." or "You just wanted to..." as these statements assume knowledge of the other person's feelings and motives. Own your feelings; avoid saying things like, "You made me sad." Use "I" messages, for example, "I feel sad when I think you are mad at me." Also, avoid saying things like, "I know how you feel." Try to change the following to "I" messages:

You do that to get on my nerves.

You are always nagging me. I'd do better if you stopped nagging.

It is also important to keep communication a two-way process. Don't monopolize; allow the other person a chance to respond while they can remember what is on their mind. Ask for feedback, for example, "Please tell me what you understood me to say." If the person did not understand, it allows you to rephrase the statement in a way that insures understanding.

Another aid to good communication is to stay on the subject. If possible, organize your thoughts ahead of time. Discuss one topic at a time and don't bring up issues that are already settled. Also, avoid "kitchen sinking," bringing up every problem and issue at one time.

Finally, good listening is an important part of communication. Give the person your full attention rather than rehearsing what you are going to say next. Let your posture, tone, and expression indicate that you are listening. Don't interrupt the person. If you are not sure you understand what the person said, ask them to clarify it. Paraphrase what they said and ask if that is correct. If not, ask then to restate it.

Good communication is essential part of recovery, and will also be helpful as we prepare to examine the next Principle of the Positive Path.

X: Principle #6
Restore connection with significant people and make connection with others who can support recovery.

Some relationships may have become strained while you were in active addiction; others may have been damaged beyond repair. It is important to try to restore those that you can and be able to let go of the ones that you can't. There will be some relationships that you will not want to maintain in recovery, as they may be harmful to your sobriety.

Family relationships are very important. These should be your first priority. You should be aware, however, that people close to you might have lost trust as a result of your past actions. As much as they might want to believe that things will be different, they are all too aware of past promises of sobriety. It may take time to restore the trust that is needed for intimacy. Be patient, and let your actions speak for you.

There may be friends that have fallen away from you during your active addiction. These people may have cared about you but they slowly became frustrated with your continued use of drugs or alcohol. You need to contact these people to apologize for any harm that you caused them in the past; let them know that you are now working on your recovery and that you would appreciate their support and friendship. Some people may not be able or willing to renew the friendship; you should be prepared for this. Others however may be glad to restore their friendship and to support your recovery. As I mentioned earlier, some friendships have been based upon our addictive use of substances; these relationships are best abandoned.

Relationships with supervisors and coworkers may have also suffered as a result of your drug use. Again, the best approach is to apologize for the damage that was caused by your use and to ask for their support of your recovery.

Take some time to reflect on the important relationships in your life. In the spaces below, list them in the appropriate space below:

Relationships that are important to my recovery:

Relationships I would like to continue if possible:

Relationships that can hurt my recovery:

In addition to restoring important existing relationships, you also need to connect with new people who can support recovery. I feel that 12 step meetings, such as Alcoholics Anonymous (AA) or Narcotics Anonymous (NA), can be an excellent source of support for recovery. While some people in these meetings tend to be very dogmatic about the program, many wonderful people attend these meetings; people who are committed to attaining and maintaining sobriety. In the Additional Information section at the rear of the book there is a chapter that discusses how to relate the Positive Path to the Twelve Steps. Many twelve-step groups also sponsor social functions such as dances and coffeehouses that offer a sober social environment.

You can also find new relationships through special interest groups, such as writers groups, through churches, places like the Ethical Society, social actions groups, and other similar organizations. It is important to remember, however, that people in these groups may be social (or addicted) users of alcohol or other drugs. Don't put yourself in a situation that could lead to a return to use. (This will be explored further in the next chapter.)

As you work on restoring and making connections with others you will find the easiest way to approach any relationship is to treat others in the same way that you would want to be treated. The hardest way may be to treat others in the way they would want to be treated. You should try to do both. Respect people who have differing points of view, even if you cannot agree with them. By listening to the feelings and needs of others, we learn more about others as well as ourselves.

XI: Principle #7
Identify barriers to recovery and plan to overcome them.

In the very first principle we talked about committing to abstinence. This is, of course, much easier to say than to do. Principles Two through Six deal with ways to sustain abstinence and promote self-awareness and personal growth. In addition to the skills gained in those principles, you need to recognize specific situations that could tempt you to return to alcohol or drug use.

As stated earlier in this book, a return to drug use after a period of sobriety is often referred to as a relapse, suggesting that the disease has again become active. There are several things that I feel you need to understand as we look at the issue of relapse.

First, you should recognize that relapse is possible but should also understand that it is not inevitable. In other words, you should be aware of the possibility but should not obsess about it. When you concentrate too much on relapse, you can mentally set yourself up for failure. When you concentrate on recovery, you maintain a positive focus; if you concentrate on relapse, you have a negative focus.

Secondly, you should be aware of the difference between a relapse and a slip. A slip is a one-time use of a mood-altering chemical. The obvious danger is that it can lead to a full return to addictive use. The important word in the last sentence is "can." A slip does not have to develop into a relapse. If you begin to blame and shame yourself for a slip, you can set yourself up for a full relapse. If, however, you can tell yourself that it was an error in judgment that you do not want to repeat, you have a better chance of getting quickly back on track.

When looking at barriers to recovery, often referred to as relapse triggers, the common list is "people, places, and things." The following exercises will look at ways to identify these various barriers and to help you develop ways to deal with them.

People

Some of the people who play a significant role in your life are people who also use mood-altering substances. It is difficult to maintain abstinence when you are around others who are using drugs or alcohol. It is too easy to be drawn back into use, especially during the early recovery period. Very often, people who are still using drugs or alcohol feel threatened by your sobriety and will encourage you to return to use. These people may be friends, family, or coworkers. You can separate yourself from some of these people; others may play an important role in your life, such as spouses, relatives, and co-workers.

The following exercise can help you to look at the people in your life who use mood-altering substances and to evaluate how to deal with them.

List all people who use mood-altering substances and who play a significant role in your life:

List those who can be avoided or eliminated from your life:

List those who you cannot avoid or eliminate:

How can you adjust your relationship with them to prevent them from hurting your recovery?

Who are positive people who can support your recovery?

Places

There may be places that had a significant role in your use of drugs or alcohol. Some may be obvious, such as bars and clubs; others may have more subtle associations, such as school, work, or other places where you often used mood-altering substances. Some may be easy to stay away from, others may not. The following questions will help you to determine places that may affect your recovery and to think of ways to deal with them.

What places do you associate with alcohol or drug use?

Which of these places can you easily stay away from?

Which of these places can not be avoided?

What can you do to maintain your recovery while you are in these places?

What are new places that will support your recovery?

Things

There are a number of "things" that can possibly lead to relapse. There may be sounds or smells that you associate with our use of substances. There may be situations that will make you crave the high you got from your drug. There may be feelings that are closely associated with using drugs. These are the things that can threaten your sobriety if you are not prepared for them.

What situations usually accompanied drug use?

Are there sights, sounds, or other things that make you think of drugs?

Choose several of these and develop ways to deal with them. (Avoidance, building new associations or reactions, etc.)

What are new things you can add to your life to support recovery?

Attitudes and Beliefs

While people, places, and things are frequently identified as relapse triggers, I feel that attitudes and beliefs are perhaps the biggest obstacles that a person in recovery has to overcome. As I have stated before, behaviors are affected by feelings and feelings are affected by what we think. There are a number of ways that attitudes and belief can make a person vulnerable to relapse. In each case, I will present the attitude or belief as well as ways to dispute them. I would like to acknowledge that some of the information here is found in the book, <u>Rational Emotive Therapy with Alcoholics and Substance Abusers</u>, by Albert Ellis, et al. Again, it is important to remember that it takes time to overcome these old beliefs. Be patient with yourself and the process.

If you have the attitude that abstinence from drugs and alcohol is a curse, you will find that recovery is a burden and you will quickly return to using. If, on the other hand, you decide that abstinence is an opportunity to improve your life you will find that recovery is much easier. If you find yourself faced with this attitude, tell yourself that you are making a choice to improve the quality of your life and you do not need mood-altering substances in your new life.

Another attitudinal barrier to recovery is self-pity. If you feel sorry for yourself because other people can use substances "responsibly" and you can't, you may decide it is all too unfair and you are going to use no matter what the consequences may be. This happens more often than you may imagine. If this is happening to you, you may tell yourself that other people do a lot of things that you cannot do, but that what matters is all the things that you *are* able to do, including living a clean and sober life.

Some people will think, "Drinking and/or using drugs isn't a problem for me. It's other people who have a problem with the way I drink and use." The way to combat that is to tell yourself "If my drinking or using is a problem for others, it soon will be for me if it is not already a problem."

Another common attitude is that sobriety will be too hard, and you might lose your friends, be bored, or be uncomfortable. To combat this attitude, remind yourself that while it may take some time and effort, you may lose much more if you continue to use.

Feeling as though you cannot stand to not have another drink or drug is another common attitude that can hurt recovery. You need to admit to yourself that abstinence is difficult, but you have endured other difficulties in the past. Also remind yourself that while you may *want* another drink or drug, you don't *need* to have it.

On a sheet of paper, in this book, or in a journal, identify some of the attitudes that may impede your recovery and lead to relapse, then develop a way to dispute the attitudes. Take time to consider both the attitudes and possible ways that you can dispute them.

My attitude:

How I can dispute that attitude:

Another attitude:

How I can dispute that attitude:

XII: Principle #8
Let Go!

The final principle consists of two simple words that carry a lot of meaning. What does it mean to let go and what are you letting go?

To begin with, you are learning to let go of feelings of guilt and shame that trap you in your addictive behavior. By taking responsibility for your actions and accepting forgiveness for them, you can release any guilt and shame. The past becomes the past and you can live in the present moment--free from any mood-altering substances.

You also let go of the compulsive desire to control the uncontrollable and to change the unchangeable. To paraphrase a familiar recovery saying, you accept what you can't change, change what you can, and you learn to understand the difference. You can't change what other people do, for instance, but you can change how you react to it.

You also let go of judgment of yourself and others. You learn to accept yourself as you are, at this moment, knowing that you are on the path of recovery.

Finally, you let go of identifying yourself with your addiction. The focus changes from "what I was" to "what I am." After years of sobriety, once the craving has been quieted, the recovering person can close the door on the past. This is not saying that a person can return to "responsible using;" in most cases any use at all could quickly lead to a full relapse. What is recommended is that the person build an identity that no longer needs their drug of choice as an identifier. This is the process of removing the drug from the self-concept.

What do you need to "Let Go" to improve your life and your recovery?

What can you do to make this happen?

Now that we have explored the basics of Positive Path Recovery, we will go on to look at a variety of ways to aid the process of building recovery.

Section Three:

The Recovery Toolbox

XIII: Recovery Is A Process

When you decide that it is time to eliminate alcohol and other drugs from your life, you want to put them down and have your life become magically normal. Unfortunately, this doesn't happen. In truth, the early months of the recovery process can be quite trying. You may suffer from Post-Acute Withdrawal, commonly referred to as PAW. While many are familiar with the acute withdrawal symptoms that are associated with some drugs, people are often unaware that there is another process that is going on in the brain and body when people stop using.

Since mood-altering chemicals mimic natural brain chemicals, your system becomes unbalanced when you flood it from drug use. The time it takes for your body and brain to re-adjust from using is considered PAW. During this period, you may experience mood swings, intense depression, lack of energy or motivation, sleep difficulties or a number of other symptoms. You need to recognize that these are normal and will lessen with time. Unfortunately, many people become impatient with the healing process and revert back to drug use to feel better.

Another part of the recovery process is becoming aware of the effect that your addiction had on your thoughts and behaviors. You need to determine how your thinking and actions were affected and eliminate the negative thoughts and behaviors while you replace them with positive ones. This takes time and work.

You will not become the person you want to be overnight; change takes time. As long as you are in the process and are moving forward, where you are today is okay for today. You need to be patient with the process.

XIV: Practicing Patience

I have often heard it said that addiction is a disease of impatience, and I certainly must agree. There is the desire for instant gratification that helps the disease to progress. If people needed to wait a long period of time to feel the effect of a drink or drug, chances are they may never have done enough of it to get addicted. It is the sudden mood swing that grabs a person and keeps them coming back. After they become hooked on this mood swing, it is hard to be patient with the process of recovery.

I often tell folks that addiction, like recovery, is a process. The difference is that the process of addiction starts out as fun and becomes work, while the process of recovery starts out as work and becomes fun. As discussed in the previous chapter, in the early stages of recovery you face Post Acute Withdrawal as well as other consequences of your addiction such as financial, legal, and relationship problems. These relationships may be family, work, or other relationships. As you face these problems in early recovery, you want the same instant relief from them that the drug provided. Unfortunately, there is no instant relief. By definition, a process takes time. you need to learn to take the time and let things grow and build.

I would like to point out that impatience is not limited to addiction; ours is an impatient society. I remember, when I was a kid, that to get a paper from my home on the East Coast to California took time and effort. I would need to put it in an envelope, put a stamp on it, and take it to the mail box. Several days to a week later it would arrive in California. Now, I take that piece of paper to the fax machine, dial a number, press send and the information goes almost immediately to California. Yet, I stand there complaining that the fax machine is slow. If you combine the impatience of our society with the impatience of addiction, there is a lot to overcome.

The only "cure" for the problem is to re-train the mind to be patient. You need to remind yourself that many things do take time. You need to remember that anything worth having is worth waiting for. You need to practice patience. The more you work at it, the more patient you become.

I once read about the Prayer for Patience. This simple prayer states: "God, give me patience and give it to me now!" The absurdity of this makes me laugh; it also allows me to see the absurdity of my own impatience. Whenever I find my patience wearing thin, I remind myself of the Prayer for Patience.

How has a lack of patience affected your recovery?

Are there areas of your life that require more patience?

What can you do to become more patient?

XV: Progress, Not Perfection

There are many slogans in the Recovery Culture. Some of them are rather lame; others start to lose their meaning with constant repetition. There is, however, one slogan that has always been important to me. That slogan is the title of this chapter.

Recognizing the need to make progress rather than to achieve perfection is another way to learn patience. If your aim is perfection, then anything less than perfection is failure. This creates a pressure not only to become perfect, but to do it as quickly as possible, since every day you are not perfect is a day of failure. With this type of pressure, patience is impossible.

The key is to recognize the progress that you have made in your recovery. Each day of recovery brings improvement. Each day brings you closer to the end of Post-Acute Withdrawal. Each day, if you are working a recovery program, brings you closer to resolving the financial, legal, and relationship problems that were created by your addiction.

Sometimes you are not able to recognize your progress. You feel as though you are just spinning your wheels. This is when you need to stop and take a look back to see how far you have come in your recovery. Progress is sometimes so gradual that you don't recognize that it has added up to significant change.

Another way to keep track of progress is to have a person or persons that you trust as a source of information. You can use these people as a "mirror" to reflect back to you the changes you have made in your life. This is important, as it is hard to see yourself realistically. Your image of yourself is influenced by how you are thinking and feeling at the time. If you are depressed, you are likely to have a low self-image. If you are happy, you are more likely to have a higher self-image. Having someone who can serve as a mirror helps you to have a clearer view of your progress in recovery. When you recognize that you are making progress, you are more likely to continue building recovery.

It is important to recognize that there are times when you are in a "holding pattern." You are not moving forward but are not moving backward. This is natural, and should not be a cause of concern. There are times when you need to rest, when the changes you have made need to "settle in." As long as you are not moving backward, you are still making progress. If this happens for too long a period, however, you may want to look at what is going on in your life that is keeping you stuck.

How do you measure your progress?

Are there areas of your life that you would like to see progress?

XVI: The Role of Goals

Goals play an important part in the process of recovery. They provide direction and also provide a way to measure progress. Goals can also provide encouragement and inspiration. A goal can be a tool to move you forward when you feel stuck.

During the intake process at one treatment program, a question that is often asked is, "What are your goals for the next year?" A frequent answer is, "To be clean and sober." This is a good goal, but that alone may not be enough. Once it has been achieved, what is there to encourage a person to continue to achieve it?

I encourage people not to see being clean and sober as a goal to achieve but as a way to achieve other goals. If, for instance, my goal is to improve my relationship with my wife and children, then being clean and sober is a way to meet that goal. Not staying sober prevents me from meeting that goal.

It is important to have both short-term and long-term goals. A long-term goal gives direction and inspiration. When you know what you want and what you have to gain, you are more likely to work to achieve it. A long-term goal can provide a "reason for being."

Short-term goals, however, give a sense of accomplishment. When you reach a short-term goal, you are able to measure your progress. A short-term goal keeps you from feeling overwhelmed and frustrated.

When you set goals, there are some things that you should keep in mind. One important thing is to be sure your goals are realistic. If you set impossible goals, you are setting yourself up for failure. If my goal is to be a multi-millionaire it might be hard to achieve, but if my goal is to be financially sound it will be easier to achieve. A reasonable goal provides encouragement rather than frustration.

You should also remember to make sure your goals apply to you and not to other people. You can change yourself but cannot change anyone else. If you set a goal of getting your spouse to love you again, you may easily fail. If, on the other hand, your goal is to be nicer to your spouse, that is achievable, even if he or she is not receptive. Keeping goals within the scope of your abilities makes them an inspiration rather than a frustration.

I have learned that it is best for me to break larger goals into a number of short-term goals. For a number of years I would travel from Maryland to visit Carol's family in Massachusetts. At first, I would think about the trip ahead; four hundred miles of driving. It would seem overwhelming and I would have trouble getting myself started. I then decided to break it down into short-term goals. I started the trip as a drive to the Delaware Memorial Bridge. From there, I drove to the New Jersey Turnpike, then to the Garden State Parkway, on to the Tappan Zee Bridge, and so on. Rather than feeling overwhelmed by the entire trip, I would feel good about having already reached a milestone. This did not decrease the length of the trip, but it changed how I felt on the trip.

Setting a series of short-term goals helps to measure progress, to feel a sense of accomplishment, and, eventually, allows you to achieve the long-term goals you have set. When you achieve goals, you are more likely to set new goals. This keeps you moving forward in your recovery.

Name at least one long-term goal.

What short-term goals will help you to achieve the long-term-goal?

How will you measure your progress?

XVII: Reward Yourself

When you think about it, addiction is based on a reward system; people use the drug and are "rewarded" with the desired mood change. It stands to reason, therefore, that you need to set up a new reward system to give yourself incentive to make difficult changes in your life. Rewards, after all, are what help people to attain their goals.

Rewards can be achieved at many levels. There is the feeling of satisfaction that comes from completing a task or meeting a goal. There is also the growing sense of health and happiness that is the result of our growing recovery. These rewards are great, but are also somewhat abstract. You may need more immediate and concrete rewards as well.

It can be difficult to find ways to reward yourself, especially in early recovery. I remember a cartoon in which the character was proud of having gone a month without chocolate. The reward was, of course, to have some chocolate. You have probably done something similar to this at some time in your life. You need to recognize that you cannot reward progress by taking a step backward.

Another pitfall is to reward yourself in a way that may add to your difficulty or cause different problems in your life. If you are facing financial difficulty in early recovery, a reward that costs a lot of money may be counter-productive. Rewarding yourself with another potentially addictive activity may also add to your problems. It is not unusual for a person recovering from alcohol or drug addiction to begin another habit. Overeating and excessive gambling or spending is commonly seen in early recovery. The reward should not be harmful to you.

So, how can you reward yourself? First, think of what you most enjoy, what you have lost in your addiction that you would like to regain, or what would be nice to try that you have never done. This can vary from person to person. You might allow yourself an hour of time to read, or to just relax, when you achieve a goal. You might promise yourself a new CD, or a trip to the movies. A dinner out, by yourself, or with family, could be nice if it doesn't strain your resources. The important thing is for the reward to be something you desire and would be willing to work for. It should be just exotic enough that it is different from your day to day experiences. It is also important to plan the reward as you plan the goal. If you know what you will get by meeting your goal, you will tend to be more focused on meeting the goal.

If you can, get others involved in setting the reward. If someone important to you is willing to assist in rewarding you there is a sense of being loved and appreciated as well as the feeling of improving a relationship that may have been damaged by the years of addiction.

I find that having a reward planned is an important part of my motivation for change. When I decided that I needed to lose weight, for instance, I promised myself a new suit when I reached my goal weight. Not only did this motivate me to lose weight, it also motivated me to maintain the weight loss. After all, once I got that new suit I needed to be able to continue to wear it.

A good reward makes a goal worth the effort it takes to achieve it. Take time to find the rewards that will keep you motivated and help you to build your recovery.

What goals do you have that will benefit from a reward?

What will the reward be?

How will you know you met the goal?

XVIII: Staying Focused

We are constantly hearing that modern society has resulted in people with short attention spans. We tend to get easily distracted and find it difficult to keep our attention on any one thing for too long. While we could debate the reasons for this, I think that we really can't debate that staying focused is harder to do in our current society. Add to this societal problem the fact that years of alcohol and drug use also affects your ability to concentrate and you can see that staying focused on recovery may be a challenge.

What can you do to stay focused? One easy thing is to "stay in the moment." It is so easy to start thinking ahead of the months and years that you will need to be alcohol and drug free that you then become focused on all the wrong things. Again, the adage, "One Day At A Time," is more than a cliché. I can more easily stay focused on what I am doing today than I can on what I will do ten years from now.

Another way to maintain focus is to stay aware of your goals and the rewards that come from meeting those goals. When that momentary thought of "why am I doing this" comes, being focused on what I am trying to achieve keeps me from getting off track.

Surrounding yourself with positive influences is another way to stay focused. When the people, places, and things in your life support recovery, you are better able to keep your focus on recovery. If, on the other hand, you keep yourself surrounded by negative influences, you are more likely to have your focus wander in the wrong direction.

Positive self-talk is another way that you can keep your focus. The first affirmation of the "New Life Acceptance Program," developed by Women for Sobriety, states, "I have a life-threatening problem that once had me." I like this, because it indicates taking charge of your life, and making change to allow this to continue. You also need to watch negative self-talk. I feel that the two most dangerous words in our language are "I can't." I do not feel that we can do anything, but I do believe that, once we tell ourselves we can't do something, we have guaranteed that we can't do it. There is one place, however, where you should use "I can't" in your recovery. You need to remember, " I can't ever use alcohol or drugs without causing more trouble in my life."

Gentle reminders of what you are trying to do in your life can also help you to stay focused. Some people may cover their car bumper with recovery stickers, some might have a copy of the Serenity Prayer hanging on the wall; others find more subtle, personal reminders. An AA token or NA keychain, hidden in a pocket, can be a great reminder to maintain focus.

Do you have trouble staying focused?

What tools can you use to keep focused?

XIX: Staying Connected

Another way to stay focused on recovery is to stay connected with people who support recovery. Meetings and other recovery related events are important to maintaining recovery. It is all too easy, however, to start feeling as though you have moved beyond the need to continue this support. You can begin to feel as though you have the tools you need and are ready to go it on your own. For many, however, this is when recovery begins to falter.

Why is this connection so important? I have found that there are many different ways that having connection with recovery groups or other people in recovery keeps our recovery growing; not all apply to everyone, but everyone will find one or two that apply.

One obvious way that this connection allows you to continue to build your recovery is that it reminds you that recovery is an ongoing process. While recovery-related thoughts and behaviors become more natural to you, old addictive thoughts and behaviors will still linger. If you are connected, you are more likely to be aware of these old ways and can quickly act to overcome them.

Another advantage to being connected is that other people can see when you are starting to be drawn into the old, addictive patterns, usually way before you may see it yourself. When you have people in your life who know addiction and recovery, you have mirrors who can reflect back to you what you do not want to see, but need to see.

Staying connected also keeps your recovery fresh. You meet new people, get new ideas, and also learn to see how your recovery is not only about being comfortable with yourself; it is about being comfortable with others. You learn that you can reach out to others while you benefit yourself. This will help you to continue to build and maintain recovery.

Staying connected also gives you structure. As much as people may complain about it, structure is important in our lives. Structure comes in many forms. People get (hopefully) structure in family rules as they grow up, structure in school, and structure at work. In active addiction, your life become structured around drug use. You need the same type of structure to be successful in your recovery. Staying connected helps you to maintain that structure.

The level of connection needed may vary from person to person and from time to time. Some may find they need to attend meetings on a daily basis, others may find that once a week is enough. The important thing is to learn to recognize your needs and feelings to determine the right amount of connection for yourself.

Take some time to consider those connections you have, and to consider connections that could aid your recovery.

What sources of connection are available to you?

Do you maintain this connection?

How can you improve your connection?

XX: You Are Not Your Addiction

After years of active addiction, it is easy to believe that the addiction is who you are. The fact is, the addiction may control you, but it does not define you. If you can recognize this difference, it becomes easier to move away from the addiction.

How many times have you told yourself that you need (or want) your drug of choice, even though you really have made a decision to quit? While you have committed to recovery, there is something inside of you that seems to want to pull you down and back to active using. This is the addiction speaking to you. If you can recognize that this thought is not coming from you but from the addiction, it becomes easier to take action against that thought. Instead of thinking, "I want to use," the thought becomes "It wants to use." The next step is to ask yourself why you should give "It" what "It" wants.

Also, when you recognize that you are not your addiction, you realize that, while you are responsible for your actions, you acted not on your beliefs and values, but on the beliefs and values of the addiction. When you learn to separate yourself from your addiction, you gain control of your thoughts and actions. The exercises in chapter six help you to connect with the true self and disconnect from the addiction.

Do you have trouble separating yourself from your addiction?

If you do, what can you do to improve this?

If not, what is helping you to keep the separation?

XXI: Wherever You Go, There You Are

Many times, people put their faith in a "geographical cure." They believe that, if they move from certain people or places, they will be able to stop using drugs and alcohol. Most of the time, this does not work. The reason it does not work is that they have carried the main problem with them – the addicted thoughts and behaviors.

As much as you may try, you cannot run away from yourself. The way to overcome the addicted thoughts and behaviors is to recognize them, then work to replace them with positive, recovery-related thoughts and behaviors. You need to recognize that these don't go away on their own. They have been a part of you for quite a while and it will take time and effort to dig them out and to get rid of them. The roots of these thoughts and actions are deep; the process of eliminating them can be slow. The rewards, however, make the effort worthwhile.

No matter what you do, or where you go in life, you will have to live with yourself. Taking the time and effort to separate yourself from the addiction will assure that you have a life that is fulfilling and worthwhile.

Are you trying to change your environment or are you changing yourself?

What steps are you taking to change yourself?

XXII: The Importance Of A Program

Have you ever purchased a product that needs to be put together? If so, did you follow the instructions or just do it "your way?" If you did it your way, did it come out all right, and did it hold up? Were there many leftover parts?

Many people think that they can do recovery "their way." While this works for some people, at least for a while, chances are that there are things that missing and the recovery is liable to collapse with time. When you have a program, you have knowledge of what you are creating, how the pieces come together to create recovery, the tools you need to create it, and the steps to take to build the recovery.

The Twelve Steps of Alcoholics Anonymous, the Eight Principles of Positive Path Recovery, and other recovery programs offer blueprints for recovery. They state what you need to build recovery and tell you how to go about doing it. In addition, they provide help and encouragement as you go through the process.

I know of a person who went about recovery "his" way. He decided that alcohol was a problem in his life and that he needed to stop drinking. He made the decision to stop drinking, and he was able to maintain his abstinence. However, as was stated early in this book, there is a big difference between abstinence and recovery. While this person was able to maintain abstinence, his life was still chaotic. He was not financially responsible, had few interpersonal skills, could not maintain a relationship, tended to be boastful in order to hide his insecurities from himself and others. When someone suggested to him that he needed to attend some meetings, he replied that he didn't need help; he was the most together person around.

Ironically; a few weeks later, this person was sitting in a psychiatrist's office and was diagnosed with depression. As this person began therapy, he began doing the work of recovery. He is now happy, sober, and able to maintain intimate relationships in his life. While he does not attend Twelve-Step meetings, he has done, and continues to do, the work of recovery. He now has a program.

The path of recovery is not a simple one, nor is it easy. When you have a program, however, you have the tools and support needed to be successful.

What structure do you have for your recovery?

How is your structure aiding your recovery?

How can you improve it?

XXIII: Understanding Triggers

If you have ever had any treatment for addiction, or have attended Twelve-Step meetings, you have heard of relapse triggers. These are things that activate the urge to use alcohol or other drugs. Some triggers are obvious, such as being around people who are using or going to places where you used to buy drugs. Some triggers are less obvious, and can be unique to the person. To learn how to deal with a trigger, you need to have a better idea of how a trigger works.

You may have heard of the researcher Pavlov and his experiments with dogs. He would ring a bell every time he fed the dogs; the dogs would salivate when the food arrived. After time, the dogs would salivate when the bell rang, even if there was no food. The dogs became trained, or conditioned, to associate the bell with food. As a result, the sound of the bell was the same to them as the sight and smell of food.

A trigger is a reaction that you have created in your mind to a thing or event. As stated before, your triggers may be common ones, or they may be very unusual. The key to dealing with triggers is to identify them, then figure ways to deal with them.

Take time to list your triggers; things that make you think about drug use. Once you have identified them, start thinking about what you can do to deal them. Some can be easily avoided or eliminated. Others will take more work and effort.

We can look at triggers as equations. If, for instance, having money is a trigger for you, the equation would seem to read "M=U," or "Money equals Using." Yet, for many people, money is not a trigger for alcohol or drug use. The real equation is "M+B=U," or "Money plus my belief about Money equals Using." In other words, it is not the money that triggers your desire to use, but what you think or believe about the money that triggers the desire or craving.

One you understand this, a solution to dealing with this trigger is easily seen. Since money in a necessity that cannot be eliminated, you can instead change what you believe about money. Instead of thinking, "If I have money I need to use drugs," you can think, "I can use this money to do something constructive in my life." This is another application of the REBT process discussed earlier in this book. Again, changing the thinking and belief about the trigger will take time and work, but the result makes the effort worthwhile.

Make a list of possible triggers you may face.

What beliefs are a part of these triggers?

Use the tools you have gained to determine ways to deal with these triggers.

XXIV: Problem Solving

Another way to deal with triggers is through problem solving. I had a teenage client who identified watching a particular television program as a trigger since he always smoked marijuana while the show was on. He did not feel that he could give up watching the show, as it was one of his favorites. While that was debatable, it provided an opportunity to demonstrate a problem-solving approach to dealing with a trigger.

We decided to present the problem to the group. The group then began to make suggestions. Some of these suggestions were rather strange, some would provide an outcome worse than the marijuana use, others, though, seemed possible. The final decision was that watching this program would become a family event; if he watched the show with his parents, he would not be able to smoke marijuana. He would also be able to talk to them about any cravings that he experienced. His parents agreed to this approach.

The difficulty with problem solving is that most addicted people used drugs and alcohol to escape problems and saw this as problem solving. Chances are that you lack problem-solving skills. The rest of this chapter will explore several problem-solving skills and tools.

One tool that was used in the example above is brainstorming. As the old saying goes, two heads are better than one. When you work alone for a solution, your experience, imagination, and abilities limit you. When other people join in the process, you get a wider range of experience, imagination and abilities.

In brainstorming, you have people suggest any idea that comes to them, no matter how silly or far out it may seem. All ideas are written down. Once the ideas are given, the group begins to look at them to decide if they are workable, if they will produce the desired result, and if the person is able to put the idea into action. Eventually, you will select the one that seems best to you and apply it. If there is more than one possible solution, it might be good to write down the others in case the selected solution doesn't work. Surprisingly, sometimes the solution that seemed far-out or silly will prove to be the best.

Often, a problem is difficult to face because it is too large and overwhelming. If, for instance, you are facing major financial problems, it may be too scary to look at the situation; therefore, you may just ignore it. A way to deal with this is to break the problem down. Make a list of all the debts. Then you can prioritize them. What is the most important one to deal with? What is less important? Are there any bills that you can eliminate? Anything you can give up to save money?

Another step is to take action. Continuing with the last example, you can call creditors to see if you can arrange for a payment plan. Some creditors are willing to work with you as long as you make an effort. Sometimes, talking to the creditor shows that you are taking responsibility; this lets them know that you are willing to make good on your obligation. Sometimes creditors might be able to suggest resources to get help with payments.

I know a person who has periodic bouts of depression. When he is in a major depressive episode he does not keep up with housework and his apartment becomes messy and disorganized. As the depression clears, he feels overwhelmed by the amount of work needed to get the house straight. He learned to break it down into smaller portions. One day he decides to clean a corner of one room. When he is done, he may decide that he is ready and able to work on another corner. On the other hand, he may decide that he has accomplished his goal for the day and then has a feeling of accomplishment. Within a reasonable amount of time, his apartment is back to normal. If he did not break the task down, however, chances are nothing would happen.

Another problem-solving tool is asking for help. This is hard for some people to do. Many people feel that asking for help is a sign of weakness or failure. Asking for help is really a normal and natural thing to do; I see it as a sign of strength and determination. We all have different skills and abilities. When you ask for help, you expand the resources that are available to you.

Sometimes, the hardest part of problem solving is deciding the right course of action. In recovery, you may face some tough decisions. You may need to consider whether to change jobs, or may need to consider ending a significant relationship. Before you can decide how to solve the problem, you need to decide what the solution should be. A great tool for this is a decision grid.

To make a decision grid, take a piece of paper and draw lines to divide it into quarters. For this example, we will look at deciding whether to change jobs. In the top left grid, write "Advantages of Staying." In the top right, put "Disadvantages of Staying." The bottom left grid would be "Advantages of Changing" and the bottom right, "Disadvantages of Changing." Now that the grid is prepared, make a list of everything you can think of for each category. For most major decisions, I suggest that you return to it several times over a period of several days or longer. Each time you go over the list, see if you still agree with the things you listed and add to the list as you think of new things.

Now you are ready to look at the grid and evaluate the information. You may have a number of entries under one or two columns and have other columns with few entries. That might indicate what the proper decision would be. On the other hand, you have to consider the quality of entries as well as the quantity. This grid, however, should help you to determine your best choice.

List problems that you face in your recovery.

What can you do to solve them?

Have you asked for help or suggestions?

Use the Decision Grid to examine a decision in your life.

XXV: Weakening Worry

Worry is a major barrier to problem solving and can be a trigger. Worry is natural, and, in moderation, moves people to take action. When worry is allowed to take over, however, it becomes a problem.

One night I was scrolling through the TV channels and came across a PBS program on the subject of worry. The person in that program defined worry as "obsessing over things that will probably never happen." Since I had a tendency to worry a lot, I held on to that definition. When I evaluated all the times of worry that I could recall, I realized that 80% of the things I worried about did not happen; also, worry did not stop the other 20% from happening. It was then that I recognized that I should, and could, do something to lessen my worry.

In early recovery, there is a lot to worry about. You may be experiencing some physical problems. You may have financial difficulties. In addition, your personal relationships might be strained. With all of this to worry about, the thought of the escape that drug use offers is inviting. Rationally, you know this is not a solution, but addiction is not rational. What can you do to escape the worry without using drugs?

First, you need to remind yourself that worry will not eliminate the problem. Then you can look at the causes of worry. The physical problems may be the result of Post-Acute Withdrawal (PAW), which was discussed in an earlier chapter. You will want to meet with a doctor to discuss your problems. It is important that your doctor know that you are in the early stages of recovery from addiction. The financial problems need to be faced using some of the problem solving tools from the last chapter. The relationships will take work; you can use some of the communication tools from Chapter Nine to help; family counseling may also be needed.

The important thing to realize is worry will not relieve the situation and will only make it worse. You need to take action and then let go of the worry. This is not easy to do, but you can train yourself to do it.

Whenever I find myself starting to worry about something, I ask myself if I have begun work on changing the situation. If I haven't, I need to start to do something about the situation. If I have, I then ask myself if there is anything that worrying about the situation will accomplish. If the answer to that is no, I make myself lay the situation aside.

I needed to learn to do this. I visualized putting the problem in a basket outside my door, telling myself I would pick it back up when I had the tools to deal with it. I also remind myself that, as long as I am doing something about the problem, worrying will not accomplish anything. With time, I have become good at doing this. You can do the same.

Are there things that cause you to worry?

Are you taking steps to deal with the sources of worry?

What can you do to ease your worry?

XXVI: Learn From The Past

Earlier in the book we looked at relapse as a process, and stated that using the drug is the end of that process. If you attempted to stop using drugs and alcohol in the past, you can use those attempts as a way to identify what went wrong in the past. This information lets you plan for ways to be successful in your present journey of recovery.

People tend to repeat their mistakes rather than make new ones. Chances are, when you look at past attempts at recovery, you will find repeating patterns that led to your return to addiction. This information alerts you to what may go wrong this time. Having that information, you can use the skills from this book to create a new, successful outcome.

The advantage of studying history is an awareness of where we have been and an indication of where we will go. This is true for our personal history as well. It is important to recognize that we cannot change our history but we can shape our future.

What barriers to recovery have you encountered in the past?

How can you use your recovery tools to overcome these barriers?

XXVII: The Art of Being

The art of being is an important part of building recovery; at the same time it can be the most difficult for many of us in Western culture to understand. I believe that the main reason that we have trouble with this concept is that we are raised to believe that we must strive to exist.

Both Taoism and Zen Buddhism embrace the concept of Wu Wei, which can best be translated as "non-striving." While this may seem like laziness or resignation to us, it represents great wisdom. Consider an oak tree; it does not try to be an oak tree, neither does it try to be a pine tree. It simply is an oak tree. A stream doesn't have to try to flow, it flows naturally. In the same manner, we don't have to try to be ourselves; we can simply be ourselves.

A lot of people who have disconnected from the true self have become locked in a pattern of trying to be what they think others would want them to be. After a lifetime of this, we tend to then try to be ourselves once we become aware that we are not being ourselves. The very act of trying drives us away from our true nature.

Perhaps one of the best illustrations of this point is one that I once read in a book; I believe that it was written by Alan Watts, although I have not been able to locate the original source. The author illustrated non-striving by giving the example of a pond. When the water is still, it gives a true reflection. If the water is stirred, however, the reflection in the water is distorted. When we "stir the waters" by trying to be ourselves, we actually create a distorted image of ourselves.

When I was young, a frequent carnival prize was what was called a Chinese finger trap. This was a tube about four inches long, woven from bamboo strips. You would place the index finger of each hand into the ends of this tube. When you tried to pull your fingers out of the tube, the bamboo would tighten around your fingers; you were, in effect trapped within this tiny cylinder. The trick to getting out of it was to relax and stop pulling; once you did this your fingers could easily slide out of the tube. This is a good example of the concept of non-striving.

Do you have difficulty slowing down?

What can you do to learn to relax?

XXVIII: The Role of Service in Recovery

Recovery, and the self-awareness that is an extension of it, carries certain responsibilities. We need to share our good fortune, the renewed sense of self, with other people. Recovery also prepares us for this task. It gives us a base of love and caring from which to act, it provides clarity in our thinking and our action, and it gives us the ability to communicate our care and concern in such a way as to build bridges rather than walls.

We cannot truly care for others when we are unable to care for ourselves. Action taken without self-awareness runs the risk of being ill advised and ineffective. We may have tried sincerely to help others while we were actively in addiction; some of our efforts may have been successful, but we did not meet our full potential as helpers.

The process of self-awareness allows us to better understand ourselves: who we are, what we believe, what we need, and what we want for our lives. As we become aware of our feelings and needs, and learn how to embrace ourselves as we are, we learn the importance of being patient with the views and shortcomings of other people as well. This allows us to approach those who differ with us in a more loving, accepting manner.

When we are out of touch with our feelings and needs, we are also unable to understand other people's feelings and needs. We tend to react in anger, demanding that others see things our way.

Unfortunately, human nature is such that we usually react to demands by becoming tough and inflexible. As a result, the adversarial relationship continues, and nothing changes.

Self-awareness leads us to the center of our being; the place where we recognize our connection to the universe and its inhabitants. No matter how you define this connection, the discovery of it is the discovery of your relationship to the world. When one is able to see the connection between oneself and the universe, there is a natural inclination to help preserve the world and those that live in it. Service to others becomes a vital part of everyday life.

Another way that the self-awareness of recovery affects our effectiveness in service is by giving us a focus to our efforts. There have been times in the past when I've had a clear understanding of the issues that were important to me. Other times, however, it has been harder for me to know what issues I should focus on and how I should take action on those issues. As I have learned to be more aware of my thoughts and feelings, I have become more effective in working for others. I am able to find the ways in which I can be most effective in promoting change, and I feel more empowered to do so.

Self-awareness enhances serving others through the discovery of innate talents and natural interests. We begin to see our gifts and to find ways to channel them. We also come to value these gifts and talents; this increases their power and effectiveness.

The way you serve others may vary from person to person. You may try to encourage others in their recovery from mood-altering substances or you may channel your energy for a social cause that you strongly believe in. No matter what you do, serving others will help you to maintain your path of recovery.

You might wonder how this applies to our topic of Building Recovery. I believe that, in helping others, you build your own character. You become more of the person you were meant to be and move away from the person the drug led you to be. You also develop a sense of purpose and achievement. It helps to develop a sense of self-esteem and a better self-image.

Another advantage is that it adds incentive to maintain recovery. You cannot reach out to help others if you are not taking care of yourself. You must practice what you are preaching. Helping others adds additional support to our recovery.

How are you reaching out to others?

How does this affect your recovery?

XXIX: Moving Forward

You are committed to making a major change in your life. The path of recovery is not always easy and is not always smooth, but it is better than the path of addiction. You are now moving toward a life of progress and healing.

This thing that we call recovery is nothing more than living life, even with all the ups and downs, rather than trying to live a fantasy life where everything always goes right.. The skills that you put into practice are normal life skills. The goals you set are natural human desires. You are starting to live life as it can be lived – with dignity, hope and purpose. You have everything you need to be successful; it is now up to you to put this knowledge and these skills to work and to continue to build your recovery.

Section Four:

Additional Information

XXX: The Positive Path and the Twelve Steps

In discussing the sixth Principle, it was suggested that AA and NA meetings can be an excellent place to meet people who can support your recovery. When attending these meetings, however, you need to be prepared to identify how you are "working the steps." I'll start by listing the steps; then I will explain how each step applies to the Positive Path.

1) We admitted we were powerless over alcohol -- that our lives had become unmanageable.
2) Came to believe that a Power greater than ourselves could restore us to sanity.
3) Made a decision to turn our will and our lives over to the care of God as we understood Him.
4) Made a searching and fearless moral inventory of ourselves.
5) Admitted to God, to ourselves, and to another human being the exact nature of our wrongs.
6) Were entirely ready to have God remove all these defects of character.
7) Humbly asked Him to remove our shortcomings.
8) Made a list of all people we had harmed, and became willing to make amends to them all.

9) Made direct amends to such people wherever possible, except when to do so would injure them or others.

10) Continued to take personal inventory and when we were wrong promptly admitted it.

11) Sought through prayer and meditation to improve our conscious contact with God as we understood Him, praying only for knowledge of His will for us and the power to carry that out.

12) Having had a spiritual awakening as the result of these steps, we tried to carry this message to alcoholics, and to practice these principles in all our affairs.

Step One and the First Principle are very similar. They both offer an acknowledgment that the substance has taken control of one's life and a recognition that a change needs to be made. The major difference is that the Positive Path does not use the term "powerless." While the person may not be able to control their use, they do have the power within them to stop use of the substance. This seems, on the surface, to be a major difference of opinion and outlook between the two programs. This discrepancy however will be dealt with as we discuss Step Three.

The Greater Power mentioned in Step Two is the Positive Path's true self. It is not a supernatural being, but it is greater than the superficial being that is so easily controlled by substances. Thus, a client using PPR can state that they have a Greater Power to help them.

The Third Step states that the person turns his or her "will and lives to the care of God *as we understood Him*." This is accomplished in the Positive Path when a person begins to redefine and rebuild the true self. They are allowing the power of the true self to become present in their self-image while decreasing the power of their drug of choice. This is not inconsistent with some spiritual approaches; the idea of "God within" can be found in Taoism, Zen Buddhism, and is also consistent with Quaker philosophy. This approach is, however, different from that of many people within the Twelve-Step community, and there may be people who object to it as trusting oneself instead of God. I encourage people who use the PPR approach to simply avoid argument and debate with AA/NA people who disagree with using the true self as a "higher power." This is, after all, the way they understand God.

I would like to point out again, at this point, that PPR is not an anti-spiritual program. Spiritual belief is an individual thing, and while it can be helpful in recovery, it is not a requirement. My goal is to remove the debate over spirituality from the recovery process. To that end, I discourage people from taking an adversarial position. The focus should be on recovering, not theology or philosophy.

Steps Four through Seven deal with making a "fearless moral inventory." In PPR, this is part of the process of redefining and rebuilding the true self.

This inventory, in PPR, is more than a list of errors and weaknesses. It also includes recognizing strengths, beliefs, wants, and needs. It is the process of incorporating those things into the self-image. It is also a process of taking responsibility for actions and taking the necessary steps to change those actions.

Steps Eight, Nine, and Ten are covered by the third principle. The Positive Path takes this part of the twelve-step program just a little further by allowing the person in recovery to accept forgiveness for these actions. The fourth, fifth, and sixth principles allow people to continue to take responsibility for their actions in the present.

The Positive Path equivalent of Step eleven is the ongoing process of redefining and rebuilding the sense of self. The twelfth step is not covered in the eight principles of the Positive Path, but the importance of service to others in recovery is stressed, as it is part of rebuilding the true self.

There are some differences between the two approaches. In PPR, clients are not encouraged to identify themselves as addicts or alcoholics. I feel that this identification keeps the substance as a part of the person's self-image, which complicates the process of rebuilding the sense of self. Since the custom in AA or NA meetings is to use this identification, however, I suggest that PPR people follow that custom at meetings.

Another obvious difference is the lack of spiritual terminology in PPR. Again, PPR takes these spiritual concepts and reframes and restates them in cognitive terms. If a person in a PPR program attends a Twelve-Step meeting, they should be prepared to accept the terminology of the steps. If they are unable to do so, they should look for alternative means of support. There are several other groups, including SMART Recovery and Secular Organizations for Sobriety (SOS). Unfortunately, these groups are not available in many areas, and they sometimes focus too much on their differences with AA.

XXXI: Feelings List

Accepting
Adventurous
Affectionate
Afraid
Aggressive
Agreeable
Amazed
Ambivalent
Amused
Angry
Annoyed
Anxious
Apathetic
Apprehensive
Ashamed
Attentive
Awed
Bashful
Bitter
Boastful
Bored
Calm
Cautious
Cheerful
Confused
Content
Contrary
Cooperative
Critical
Curious
Daring
Defiant
Delighted
Demanding
Depressed
Despairing
Disagreeable
Disappointed
Discouraged
Disgusted
Disinterested
Displeased
Dissatisfied
Distrustful

Eager
Ecstatic
Elated
Embarrassed
Empty
Enthusiastic
Envious
Exasperated
Forlorn
Furious
Gloomy
Greedy
Grief-stricken
Grouchy
Guilty
Happy
Helpless
Hesitant
Hopeful
Hopeless
Hostile
Humiliated
Impatient
Impulsive
Indecisive
Indignant
Intolerant
Irritated
Jealous
Lonely
Meek
Nervous
Obliging
Obedient
Panicky
Patient
Pensive
Playful
Pleased
Possessive
Proud
Puzzled
Quarrelsome
Rebellious

Receptive
Reckless
Rejected
Remorseful
Resentful
Sad
Sarcastic
Satisfied
Scared
Scornful
Self-conscious
Serene
Shy
Sociable
Sorrowful
Stubborn
Surprised
Suspicious
Sympathetic
Terrified
Timid
Trusting
Uncertain
Unhappy
Unsympathetic
Vacillating
Watchful
Wondering
Worried

XXII: Selected Readings

I refer to several books in some of the chapters. I have listed these here so that you can do additional reading on any subject that interests you. Some of these books are designed for Addiction Treatment professionals and may be too dry or technical for many people, but they do contain some good information.

Alcoholics Anonymous (The Big Book), published by Alcoholics Anonymous World Services, Inc.

Rational Emotive Therapy with Alcoholics and Substance Abusers, written by A. Ellis, J.F. McInerney, R. DiGiusepppe, and R.J. Yeager, published by Allyn & Bacon

Positive Path Recovery, written by G. Blanchard, published by Positive Path Books.

About The Author

Gary Blanchard began his career in the addiction treatment field after graduation from College of Notre Dame of Maryland's Weekend College in 1998. In 2000, Gary enrolled in Vermont College of Norwich University; he received a Masters in Addictions Counseling from Vermont College in 2002.

Since moving to West Brookfield, Massachusetts, in 2006, Gary worked in programs for people with co-occurring disorders. He also has a private practice, providing counseling in Ware, Massachusetts. Gary teaches at Holyoke Community College in Holyoke, Massachusetts. He is a licensed alcohol and drug counselor; in 2014 he was named Counselor of the Year by the Massachusetts Association of Alcohol and Drug Abuse Counselors (MAADAC).

Gary is the author of *Positive Path Recovery* and *Counseling for Medication Assisted Recovery.* He has presented at many local and national conferences. He is currently the President of MAADAC.